Vicki Rasmussen has created a wonderful book to guide parents as they help their children learn to read. Teaching reading through the cultural practices of the home is such an important support to a child's efforts to learn to read. Any educator would welcome the assistance of the home in preparing and teaching children to read. While children may well learn to read in the home from a parent using the process Mrs. Rasmussen outlines, the process outlined in her book also supports any school's efforts to teach reading. Better readers will come from homes emphasizing reading.

—Steven O. Laing, EdD
Former Utah State Superintendent of Public Instruction

Head Start

with the

Book of Mormon

The Lasley family —

May God bless your family as you read the Book of Mormon together! Hugs + wishes,

Vicki —

Head Start

with the

Book of Mormon

Using the Scriptures to Teach Children Reading and Writing Skills

by Vicki Lynn Rasmussen

CFI
Springville, Utah

ISBN 13: 978-1-59955-067-1

Published by CFI, an imprint of Cedar Fort, Inc., 2373 W. 700 S., Springville, UT, 84663
Distributed by Cedar Fort, Inc., www.cedarfort.com

LIBRARY OF CONGRESS CATALOGING-IN-PUBLICATION DATA
Rasmussen, Vicki Lynn, 1959–
  Head start with the Book of Mormon : helping children learn to read using
the Book of Mormon / Vicki Lynn Rasmussen.
    p. cm.
  Includes bibliographical references.
  ISBN 978-1-59955-067-1
  1. Book of Mormon. 2. Mormon Church—Sacred books. 3. Church of Jesus
Christ of Latter-Day Saints—Doctrines. 4. Mormon Church—Doctrines.
5. Reading (Primary) 6. English language—Study and teaching (Primary) I.
Title.

  BX8627.A2R38 2007
  289.3'22—dc22

                      2007017747

Cover design by Nicole Williams
Cover design © 2007 by Lyle Mortimer
Edited and typeset by Kimiko M. Hammari

Printed in the United States of America

10 9 8 7 6 5 4 3 2 1

Printed on acid-free paper

A great and marvelous work is about to come forth unto the children of men. Behold, I am God; give heed unto my word, which is quick and powerful, sharper than a two-edged sword.

—Doctrine & Covenants 6:1–2

Dedicated to my son, Cade,
who inspired me—
and to all the children who,
through the Book of Mormon,
will learn to read.

Contents

Foreword

When Moroni first appeared to Joseph Smith, he quoted Malachi: "And he shall plant in the hearts of the children the promises made to the fathers, and the hearts of the children shall turn to their fathers. If it were not so, the whole earth would be utterly wasted at his coming" (JS–H 1:39). Moroni added that this prophecy "was about to be fulfilled" (JS–H 1:40).

Two questions beg to be asked. First, what promises are to be planted in the hearts of the children lest the world shall be wasted? Second, how can these promises be literally planted in the hearts of our children?

Moroni's appearance to Joseph Smith provides us the answer to the first question. It was to announce the coming forth of the Book of Mormon, the very thing that "was about to be fulfilled." Indeed, Moroni's father, Mormon, explained in the preamble of the Book of Mormon that the promises that are to be planted in the hearts of the children are the covenants contained in the golden plates. He wrote that the sacred record's purpose is "to show unto the remnant of the House of Israel what great things the Lord hath done for their father; and that they may know the covenants of the Lord, that they are not cast off forever" (Book of Mormon title page). Thus, Latter-day parents are instructed "to bring up your children in light and truth" (D&C 93:40) and to "seek diligently to turn the hearts of the children to their fathers" (D&C 98:16).

However, the answer to the second question—how can parents plant the words of the Book of Mormon into the hearts of their children?—is not as readily discernible. What pedagogy can a parent use to plant in the heart of a small child the light and truth of the promises found in the Book of Mormon? This book provides an innovative and effective way to begin transmitting the word of the Book of Mormon into the hearts of our younger children.

I live in the Arabian Peninsula, where it is estimated that some ten billion birds immigrate across its vast deserts each year, returning from Africa to their breeding lands in the north. The Lord has implanted in the brain of these birds a black isometric mineral called magnetite that acts like a compass. Without the aid of the magnetite, the birds would soon become lost and perish.

Without the promises of Book of Mormon planted in the hearts of our children, they and the world they live in will perish at the Lord's Second Coming. Before we send our small children into the confusion of the temporal world, let's be sure we provide them with their own internal Liahona, the words of the Book of Mormon resounding in their hearts. The iron rod is the word of God, and for our children to hold to it, they must recognize its word. Vicki Rasmussen is an outstanding mother and talented teacher, and her technique for planting the words of the Book of Mormon into the hearts of our children is of great worth.

George Potter
Book of Mormon explorer, author, lecturer, and filmmaker

Acknowledgments

My gratitude goes first to Father in heaven for the Great Plan of Happiness and to all His holy prophets who taught it. Without their words, a book on this subject would not need to be written. Next, my gratitude goes to Jesus Christ, my eldest brother, who created the world in which I live and who rescues me from this mortal realm. I am grateful for the Holy Spirit's guidance in teaching my children to read the scriptures and in writing this book.

Much love goes to my maternal grandmother who gave me my first happy memories of being read to. Also, wherever she is, I thank my first-grade teacher, Mrs. Reddington, at Panama Elementary School, for her kindness to me, instilling within me a desire to teach others. I greatly appreciate my parents for the freedom they gave me to follow my dreams and for teaching me the importance of knowing God's will. I am ever appreciative of my husband, Mark, for his support, which allows me to pursue my own interests, and for the seven good children we have been blessed with, especially Cade, who wanted to read.

I also thank our son's kindergarten teacher, Robin Davis, for assisting us on our journey into reading. I wish to thank everyone I have tutored over the years and the teachers and parents who let me tutor their children. Continually, they taught me how to be a better teacher. From my heart, I thank all those who helped proof this manuscript: Kimiko Hammari, my editor; Sydney M. Johnson, my mother; Joy Haws, Janice Barrus, Sherilyn Tibbitts, and Teresa Woodward, amazing teachers at Century Elementary School; Karen Kuebler, who is also a mom; George Potter, friend and author; and my husband and children for their insights. My biggest thanks goes to the publishers, who believe this message will help children—and thanks to each of you who will share this program with your child.

1 Program Outline

While I was visiting friends who had young children and teenagers, one of the parents complained, "What can we do?" It was the frustrated response to a seemingly losing battle with the adversary over the welfare of our children: How do we keep our children safe from worldly temptations and the powers of darkness?

Satan would have us use his tactics, forcing our children to do right at every turn. But when our children confront temptations on their own, they need to be armed with a strength of will forged by the frequent exercise of their own agency. The best chance our children have is to grow up with as much kindness, goodness, and godliness as we can bring them. Then, when temptations to flirt with misery do come, they will recognize it for what it is.

We can show our children kindness by our actions and goodness by our examples. But how can we bring them godliness? In this mortal realm, there are at least three important ways: worship, prayer, and study.

Through worship we have occasion to commit (and recommit) ourselves to holiness, to learn, and to strengthen one another. In prayer, we open our heart to the One who loves us most and try to soften it so that guiding truths may enter there in return. Through study, we listen to and read the words of prophets, those who tried to walk the Master's road. They left for us their counsel—real heroes with practical lessons on goodness, a wisdom inspired by the Most Holy One to lift and sustain us in time of need. The prophet Joseph's translation of Matthew 1:37 reads, "Whoso treasureth up my word, shall not be deceived."

These three ways shine brighter in the lives of our children when we as parents reflect their importance in our own lives. God's strategies for the well-being of his children are the same methods necessary for parents to strengthen their children: God gave us agency at birth and makes available to us the knowledge to use it wisely. Then, when we as parents provide our children with knowledge (our own example combined with that found in the scriptures), this will arm them with the ability to make their own wise choices. When our children grow up with good examples, prayer, worshiping God, and learning His words from their youth, what could we have done more?

The Family Bible

Old man Higgins built a shelf,
For the family Bible to rest itself,
Lest a sticky finger or a grimy thumb
Might injure the delicate pages some.
He cautioned the children to touch it not,
And it rested there with never a blot,
Though the Higgins tribe is a troublesome lot.

His neighbor, Miggins, built a shelf,
"Come children," he said, "and help yourself."
Now the Miggins' Bible is ragged and worn
With some of the choicest pages torn
Where children have fingered and thumbed and read,
But of the Miggins children it is said,
Each carries a Bible in his head.
(Author unknown)

We learn from Moses that the commandment to teach our children from scripture began with Adam. God revealed to Moses that in Adam's day "a book of remembrance was kept" that was used to record those things written "by the spirit of inspiration; And *by them their children were taught to read and write*" (Moses 6:5–6; italics added). At the edge of the Promised Land, just before his death, Moses gave these special instructions:

> Love the Lord thy God with all thine heart, and with all thy soul, and with all thy might. And these words, which I command thee this day, shall be in thine heart: And thou shalt teach them diligently unto thy children, and shalt talk of them when thou sittest in thine house, and when thou walkest by the way, and when thou liest down, and when thou risest up. (Deuteronomy 6:5–7)

God revealed to Solomon, "I love them that love me; and those that *seek me early* shall find me" (Proverbs 8:17; italics added). Paul also spoke of learning scripture from childhood:

> But continue thou in the things which thou hast learned and hast been assured of, knowing of whom thou hast learned them; And that from a child thou hast known the holy scriptures, which are able to make thee wise unto salvation through faith which is in Christ Jesus. All scripture is given by inspiration of God, and is profitable for doctrine, for reproof, for correction, for instruction in righteousness: That the man of God may be perfect, thoroughly furnished unto all good works. (2 Timothy 3:14–17)

To the Romans, Paul said, "For whatsoever things were written aforetime were written for our learning, that we through patience and comfort of the scriptures might have hope" (Romans 15:4). He spoke of those who "were more noble . . . in that they received the word with all readiness of mind, and *searched the scriptures daily*, whether those things were so. Therefore many of them believed" (Acts 17:11–12, italics added). Throughout history, God's words to mankind have included the counsel to read the scriptures.

In our day, the Lord revealed that "the Book of Mormon and the holy scriptures are given of me for your instruction" (D&C

33:16). Jeffrey R. Holland of the Quorum of the Twelve Apostles (former president of Brigham Young University), said:

> As the word of God has always been—and I testify again that is purely and simply and precisely what the Book of Mormon is—this record is "quick and powerful, sharper than a two-edged sword, to the dividing asunder of both joints and marrow" (D&C 6:2). The Book of Mormon is that quick and that powerful for us. And it certainly is that sharp. Nothing in our history and nothing in our message cuts to the chase faster than our uncompromising declaration that the Book of Mormon is the word of God. On this issue we draw a line in the sand.
>
> It was the Book of Mormon that changed my life, told me the gospel of Jesus Christ has been restored, and immersed me in the Church, heart and soul. I hold it in a category sacred to me among all the world's literature. It stands preeminent in my intellectual and spiritual life, the classic of all classics, a reaffirmation of the Holy Bible, a voice from the dust, a witness for Christ, the word of the Lord unto salvation. ("True or False," *Liahona*, June 1996, 47)

In the Book of Mormon the prophet Nephi explained why what he had written was so important: "For my soul delighteth in the scriptures, and my heart pondereth them, and writeth them for the learning and the profit of my children" (2 Nephi 4:15). Just before his death he testified, "if ye shall press forward, *feasting upon the word of Christ*, and endure to the end, behold, thus saith the Father: Ye shall have eternal life" (2 Nephi 31:20; italics added).

About four hundred years later, Alma the younger ascribed his friends' faithfulness to the scriptures. As the king's sons, they had given up their right to rule the kingdom after their conversion so they could go and preach to their enemies. When Alma met up with them fourteen years later, it was recorded: "They were still his brethren in the Lord; yea, and they had waxed strong in the knowledge of the truth; for they were men of a sound understanding and they had searched the scriptures diligently, that they might know the word of God" (Alma 17:2).

Teaching our children God's powerful words can bring about "a great and marvelous work" in their lives. Five times in the Doctrine and Covenants the prophet Joseph stated, "A great and marvelous work is about to come forth unto the children of men," and followed it with what Paul told the Hebrews: "Behold, I am God; give heed unto my word, which is quick and powerful, sharper than a two-edged sword" (D&C 6:1–2). Then he continued on to promise many wonderful blessings: salvation, personal revelation, wisdom, eternal life, God's love, and peace. Growing up with regular scripture reading, our children, too, can become "sharper than a two-edged sword."

We have probably thought about reading the scriptures daily, but it is a struggle to fit it into our busy schedule. We have learned that it is important, but the language of scripture seems so difficult. Over time this becomes easier, and even if we don't understand everything we read, there are always new things to discover. It is never too late—or too early—to begin this adventure.

Two things are prerequisite to daily scripture reading: knowing how to read and developing a habit of doing it. Learning to read usually comes first, and then we develop a habit of reading daily. This program is unique because it is based on the idea that it is easier to develop a habit of daily scripture reading by learning to read using the scriptures daily.

This program has many purposes. When used to teach children to read, it will help them become competent readers, giving them a head start in education and the ability to make a way for themselves in the world. Using the program regularly will help parents encourage in their children a lifelong habit of scripture reading. Regular reading prepares children to meet life's challenges with knowledge—truths found in the gospel of Jesus Christ. These truths bring peace and faith, which in turn builds character.

This program has three phases. The first phase is designed for children who cannot read. The second phase adjusts the program to children who are beginning to read. The final phase of the program is for silent readers. This plan grows with a child and addresses the needs of children of all ages.

This program uses the Book of Mormon to teach a child reading and writing skills in a "quick and powerful" way. The steps are simple and take a short amount of time each day. The details are explained in chapter 2. Below is a brief outline:

Phase One

Scatter these activities (in any order) throughout the day:

A. Read a Storybook Together (5–10 minutes)
1. **Choose** a book with your child.
2. **Read and discuss** the pictures and story.
3. **Point out** a few letters, numbers, sounds, or words your child has already practiced using the Book of Mormon.

B. Practice One Letter (6–8 minutes). Select the lowercase and uppercase flashcard for this letter (see page 55). Upon completion of the alphabet, repeat these steps with the number flashcards, and then use the letter flashcards again to teach sounds. Select a new flashcard when your child remembers yesterday's letter (or number or sound). Repeat this cycle as a review until your child can remember them. Your child will:
1. **Point to and repeat** 10 times the letter, number, or sound, while counting on fingers and looking at the flashcard.
2. **Write and recite** the letter or number 5 times. (Then, you will each choose your favorite written examples.)
3. **Circle and recite** the letter or number 5 times when finding it in the Book of Mormon.

C. **Practice One Word** (15 minutes). Select both the lowercase and uppercase flashcard depicting the same word (included). Select a new flashcard when your child remembers yesterday's word.

1. **Review** flashcards and remove them as they are learned.
2. **Point to and repeat** the word 10 times with your child, counting on fingers.
3. **Write and recite** the word 5 times and choose favorites.
4. **Underline and recite** the word 5 times when finding it in the Book of Mormon.

Phase Two

Follow these steps (in any order) when your child knows the top 50 words in the Book of Mormon (see page 127).

A. **Read a Storybook Together** (5–10 minutes)

1. **Choose** a book with your child.
2. **Read** to your child, have your child read to you, or do some of both.
3. **Discuss** the story with your child.

B. **Read the Scriptures Together** (5–10 minutes). Gradually add verses until your child can read most of the words in one scripture column.

1. **Underline** all known words in two verses of the Book of Mormon. (Your child does this, but eventually you will do it for them.)
2. **Read aloud,** taking turns. Your child reads the words they know, and you read the words in between.
3. **Define** one new word for your child.
4. **Summarize** or discuss briefly what was read.

Phase Three

Follow these steps (in any order) when your child can read most of the words in one scripture column:

A. Read a Storybook Together (5-10 minutes).
1. **Choose** a book with your child.
2. **Read** to your child, have your child read to you, or do some of both.
3. **Discuss** the story with your child.

B. Your Child Reads Silently (you spend approximately 5 minutes with your child when they are done reading). Your child reads one page, increasing to one chapter, up to 20 minutes a day.
1. **Underline.** Have your child underline any unfamiliar words while reading.
2. **Define.** After your child is finished reading, go over any underlined words.
3. **Summarize** or briefly discuss what was read.

2 Program Details

Storybooks

No child is too young to benefit from being snuggled up and read to. Learning will become a special time when both of you enjoy being together. A child may wiggle a lot during reading time, but that is okay. Some children seem to learn better when they are moving. The first step to learning is being able to pay attention. At first a child may be able to pay attention only for a few minutes. When the routine becomes regular, is relaxed, and is fairly short, your child will enjoy the time you spend together.

Begin by looking for books with nice pictures and not many words. Be sure they are at the right level for your child. If you do not have many books, visit the library or yard sales. If your child is already in school, the teacher will probably have books that you can borrow from the classroom. If your child is not in school, his or her future kindergarten teacher may have beginning readers that you can borrow.

Choose a couple of books that are the right length for your child's attention span. This is especially helpful if your child often chooses books that are too long or can't decide on a book. After you have chosen a couple of books, let your child pick between these two. Repetition is a great learning tool, so if your child has a favorite book, read it as often as it is desired.

Encourage your child to hold the book or turn the pages. This will help keep your child occupied and focused on the book. Point out objects in the story that your child is familiar with, and talk about them. Mention things in your child's world when they relate to the story. Ask your child questions about the story. Let your child interrupt the story to ask you questions or talk about things that the story may bring to mind.

Sometime during the story ask your child to point to a letter, number, or word that they have already practiced. You may need to point out a few of them yourself. Ask your child if they know what it is, and pause for a moment to see if they remember. If your child cannot remember in a few seconds, provide the answer. This gives a gentle reminder and keeps the story moving along. When your child answers correctly, help them feel excited about being able to read! At first, do this about once every other page. Question your child periodically, but don't make the process tiresome.

Reading daily to your child just for fun is a very important part of teaching your child to read. It is necessary that your child hear you model what reading aloud sounds like. It is also good to show your child the joy that can be found in sharing a story together!

Reciting and Writing Letters

Soon after you and your child have begun the habit of reading together daily, begin teaching your child the names of letters. Start with the first letter of the alphabet, and select both the lowercase and uppercase flashcards (provided in chapter 6). It is helpful if the lowercase and uppercase letters are photocopied on two different colors of cardstock. You might let your child choose the colors, especially if color vision deficiencies are present.

Ask your child to repeat the name of the letter ten times while looking at the two flashcards. Help your child keep track by counting on your fingers each time it is recited. If your child holds the flashcards or points to the letters, this will help focus their attention on the cards. If your child already knows the name of the letter, introduce the next letter.

Now, offer your child a blank sheet of paper and a crayon or pencil. You might let your child choose whether to sit at a table or lie on the floor with a lapboard. Let your child enjoy being involved in making choices in these activities whenever possible. Have your child practice writing both of these letters five times each, using the flashcards as a model.

After writing a letter, have your child immediately recite the name of the letter. At first, let your child form the letters any way they like, and make them as large as they like. When your child finishes writing them, look them over together. Ask your child to circle their favorite lowercase *and* uppercase letter. Praise your child for their diligent efforts, and point out your favorite letters, explaining why you chose them. Choosing favorites encourages neatness and makes the activity more fun.

If your child is willing, model how each lowercase and uppercase letter is formed by writing an example of each on their paper. When your child becomes more comfortable with writing, begin the activity with a short reminder to start each letter at the top to form it correctly. Begin using lined paper when your child is confident using a pencil. Direct your child to use two lines to make each letter if you do not have paper with dotted center guidelines. This gives your child a reference line for beginning each lowercase letter. To help your child remember this, explain that the top and bottom of each letter "kiss" the line!

Finding Letters

Tell your child that they are now able to read their very own scriptures! While you are reading your scriptures, have your child look in their scriptures for the letter they have just practiced (either the lowercase or uppercase letter). Let your child use the flashcards for reference. Tell your child to circle it when they find one and to show it to you and tell you its name. Ask them to find five of them.

If your child forgets the name of a letter while looking for it in their scriptures, have them repeat its name five more times, while looking at the flashcards. A child may not be able to remember the names of letters for very long. So, periodically during the day, you may want to ask your child if they can still remember what letter they are learning.

If your child knows a letter when you first show it to them, or can remember their letter from the previous day, offer praise and introduce the next letter of the alphabet. You do not need to review the letters you have previously practiced with your child. After teaching your child numbers, you will again return and review the letters.

Most of the letters of the alphabet are easy to find in the scriptures. For instance, *V* can be found in the common word *ha<u>v</u>e*. The letter *J* is often found in the book of Jacob. Alma 19 speaks of the queen, and Mosiah and Alma write frequently of <u>Z</u>arahemla. You might also refer your child to the index of the Book of Mormon, where *X* is found in many words beginning with *E*.

Reciting, Writing, and Finding Numbers

After your child has learned the names of each letter, teach your child the names of all the numbers from 0 through 20. Select the "0" flashcard and ask your child to repeat the word *zero* ten times, while looking at the flashcard. You and your child can keep track of your count by using your fingers.

Now, have your child practice writing the number five times on a sheet of paper. Make sure your child recites the number after writing each one. For variation when writing numbers, a chalkboard or white board may be used. These boards make neatness more difficult, so have your child use paper when writing letters or words. When your child is finished, be sure that both of you pick out the number that you each think looks the best.

Next, have your child look for the number five times in their scriptures, and circle them. Your child is welcome to find the number inside a larger number. Point out to your child that there are page numbers at the top of each page and that the scriptures are divided into short verses, each beginning with a number. Show your child the chapter numbers also, and explain that there are new chapters about every other page. Help your child feel good about being able to read their scriptures too!

Each time your child finds a number, have them show it to you and recite it. If your child forgets the number while looking for it, have them repeat its name to you five more times (while looking at the flashcard). When your child can remember their number the following day, offer praise and introduce the next number. You do not need to review the numbers you have practiced previously. After reviewing letters with your child, you will return again to numbers.

Reviewing

After teaching your child the names of the numbers from 0 through 20, review the alphabet flashcards again. Go over them like before (writing them and using the scriptures), but not in alphabetical order. This time divide the flashcards into ten sets of similarly shaped letters: *a-c-e-o, b-d-g-p-q, f-i-j-l-r-t, h-m-n-u-v-w, k-x-y-s-z* (lowercase), and *C-D-G-O-Q, B-E-F-H-P-R, I-J-L-T, M-N-U-V-W, A-K-X-Y-S-Z* (uppercase). This will help your child learn to see the differences between letters that are similar.

Select one of the above sets of cards. Practice only one letter per sitting with your child. If your child can remember a letter when it is first reintroduced, select the next letter. When your child practices a letter each day, also review the other flashcards in the set that your child has already practiced this time around. Retire each set of letters when selecting the next set. Always help your child to feel good about their progress!

After reviewing the letters a second time, teach your child the numbers from 5 though 50, counting by fives. Have your child write them and use the scriptures as before. When each number is learned, add the next flashcard to the group. Each day review all the previous flashcards, in order. This will help your child learn to count by fives.

Continue reviewing letters and numbers alternately, until your child knows all of their names. Practice the numbers from

10 through 100, counting by tens. Finally, practice the numbers from 20 through 50.

Playing games with the flashcards makes reviewing them more fun. When reviewing a set of numbers, let your child try to match double-digit numbers that have the same beginning or ending number. Review the name of the matching numbers. Or, see if your child can put them in order.

Your child may also enjoy a matching or memory game with the alphabet cards. Mix up a set of lowercase and uppercase cards that your child is reviewing. (If the lowercase and uppercase cards are printed on different colored cardstock, first have your child divide the cards into two sets.) Spread them face up on a table or the floor.

Help your child turn all the letters right-side up. Now, see if your child can find a matching lowercase and uppercase card. Point out the similarities between the two letters. See if your child can name the letter. If not, have your child repeat its name to you five times, while looking at the flashcard.

Reciting, Writing, and Finding Sounds

After you have taught your child the names of the letters and numbers, use the letter flashcards again to teach your child sounds. Select the vowel flashcards used previously to teach the short vowel sounds.

Additional flashcards are provided in chapter 6 to teach letters with multiple sounds. The flashcards that teach the long vowel sounds are printed with a line above the letter (including /y/ as in *my*). All irregular sounds are printed with a line underneath the letter: /a/ in *also*, /c/ in *city*, /g/ in *gentile*, /o/ in *of*, /o/ in *who*, /s/ in *is*, /u/ in *put*, /x/ in *Xerxes*, and /y/ in *many*. A word is printed on the back of these cards to help you teach the correct sound. These words were chosen for their occurrence in the Book of Mormon.

When you begin teaching your child sounds, teach the consonants that have only one sound first. (This excludes *c, g, s, x,* and *y*). As before, select a letter (both the lowercase and uppercase flashcard) and teach one sound at a time. Do not review the name of a letter with your child when teaching the sounds. Have your child recite just the sound, ten times, and then write the letter five times, repeating its sound again when writing them. Make sure both of you choose your favorite uppercase and lowercase letters. Then, have your child find and circle their letter five times in their scriptures (either lowercase or uppercase), show it to you, and recite its sound again each time.

Next, teach your child the sounds of the consonants *c*, *g*, *s*, and *x*, one at a time. These letters have two sounds. Teach them one at a time, but consecutively. Finally, teach your child the various vowel sounds: two sounds for *e* and *i*, three sounds for *u* and *y*, and four sounds for *a* and *o*. (To teach the fourth sound for *a*, use the flashcard included with the word cards.) Learning the various letter sounds will provide your child with the means to figure out new words all on their own!

Reciting, Writing, and Finding Words

Soon after you and your child have made a regular habit of practicing letters, begin teaching words. Your child can learn words before knowing all the names and sounds of letters. Learning words will teach your child the importance of knowing letters.

On page 127, you will find a handy reference chart. These are the 50 words you will need to teach your child. They are listed in the order to be taught. Flashcards for these words are also found in chapter 6. Each word is included twice (except for the word *I* and proper names). On one card the word is printed in lowercase letters, and on the other card the word begins with a capital letter.

Place the first word in front of your child. Explain that the word is the same on both cards. If your child has already learned the beginning letter of the word, review that both the lowercase and uppercase letters are the same. Have your child repeat the word ten times, while looking at the cards. Use your fingers to keep track of your counting.

Now, have your child practice writing the word five times on a sheet of paper. Have your child recite the word after writing each one. Make sure your child practices copying both flashcards (the lowercase and the uppercase word) five times each. When your child is finished, remember to choose favorites.

Next, have your child look for their word (either lowercase *or* uppercase) five times in their scriptures. Have your child underline each one, show it to you, and recite it. Your child may like to keep track of how many times they have found a word by making little tick marks at the top of their page. If your child forgets the word while searching for it, have them repeat it to you five more times, while looking at the flashcards. Help your child enjoy playing scripture Hide and Seek, or Word Find!

If your child underlines the wrong word, be positive. Ask your child to check the word more closely. After searching briefly, your child may want your help to find their word. You may want to use a three-minute sand timer. Tell your child that when the sand runs out, you will help them find the word.

When you need to help your child find a word, browse through several pages in their scriptures. Some words are used more often in some books than others, so flip around. It is good to model for your child that sometimes it takes longer to look for a word than at other times. By your example your child will learn to be more patient. Your child might enjoy looking for the word too, seeing who can find it first. (As a last resort, check chapter 5 for at least 50+ references for each of the words.)

When you find your child's word for them, tell them the verse number where you found it. This hint will give your child a chance to practice using numbers. If your child has trouble finding the verse number, tell them which page or column it is in. If your child has not yet learned this number, or has forgotten it, be sure to say the number when you point to it. Now that your child knows which verse their word is in, have them finish finding it.

If your child is able to read a new flashcard when it is first presented, or remembers their word from the previous day, give praise and introduce the next word. Each day, also review all the words that have been practiced thus far. You may enjoy reviewing these words by playing a memory or matching game with the lowercase and uppercase cards. When your child reads a word easily, retire that card from further use.

Reading

After your child has learned the top 50 words found in the Book of Mormon, begin reading the Book of Mormon together. Each day have your child underline the words that they know in only two verses. Show your child these verses by circling their verse numbers. Then, read aloud, taking turns. Your child will read the underlined words, and you will read the words in between.

When your child is consistently able to remember the top 50 words, you can underline your child's words to speed up the process. If you decide to do so, simply underline them while you are reading along. This way your child will know when it is their turn to read. Occasionally underline an additional word that you think your child will be able to sound out. At first, select only one new word per verse.

You will not need to underline your child's words when their reading improves. However, it is handy to use a pencil or other pointer to identify the words you want read. Let the pointer rest on a word until you get to the next word you want your child to read. This helps to keep your child from trying to sound out the wrong words. Remember to go over the meaning of one new word each day.

Add another verse to your daily reading when your child can easily follow your pencil or pointer. At this stage, take a moment when you are finished reading to briefly summarize what was read in a couple of sentences, with simple words. When your child's reading improves, occasionally have them tell you what was read. Continue to discuss the meaning of one new word each day. Gradually add verses until you and your child can read a whole scripture column together!

When your child can read most of the words in one scripture column, they can begin to read silently at the rate of one page per day. When finished reading, have your child circle their page number to keep track of where they have read. Always make sure your child underlines any words they don't know. Go over these words together after your child has finished reading. Then, ask your child to tell you briefly about what was read.

Gradually increase your child's reading to twenty minutes, or one chapter, whichever comes first. Eventually your child will be able to read a chapter each day, even if it is a long one. Have your child put the date next to each chapter they have completed. Dating the pages will be useful if your child's school requires extra reading to be done at home. Your child will also enjoy being able to see quickly how much they have read.

Rereading Words

The habit of rereading will help improve your child's reading skills. Decoding is the ability to put several sounds together to form a word. Rereading a word reinforces your child's decoding skills. Comprehension is the ability to understand the meaning intended by the writer. Rereading phrases or sentences improves comprehension and builds your child's fluency. Fluent reading sounds like speech. It includes reading effortlessly, pausing appropriately, using expression, and reading words accurately.

A conscientious learner will instinctively reread passages when needed. The suggestions below will encourage your child to make a habit of doing this. When your child automatically rereads when needed, they are becoming a self-learner and an independent reader.

Rereading words read correctly: When your child first begins to sound out words, make sure this is done aloud. This will help you know if a particular letter is confusing your child. Some children like to sound words out loud for a very long time. This is fine. Let your child linger at each stage in their reading development for as long as they feel it necessary to do so.

When your child reads a word correctly but sounds it out very slowly, ask your child to reread the word. Your child may do this automatically. This will help your child build decoding skills.

Rereading words misread: When your child practices or reviews individual words on flashcards, a word may be misread. Pause for a moment to see if your child automatically corrects the word. If not, repeat the word your child just said. For example, if the word was *yea*, you might ask, "Did I hear *ye?*" This will prompt your child to check the word.

If your child is unsure of the word, point to the letter that was misread. Ask your child to tell you its sound. (You may need to remind your child to try another sound for a particular letter.) If your child cannot remember the correct sound for a letter after a short pause, tell it to your child. This keeps things moving. A child may not want a sound or a word told to them. They want to figure it out themselves. However, most children will tire of having to guess repeatedly.

Now that your child knows the correct sound, ask them to try the word again. After a short pause, or if your child again misreads the word, tell your child the word. Then, ask your child to repeat the word on the flashcard five times.

When a word is misread, your child may have added an extra sound that was not there. In this case there is not a misread letter that you can point to. If the word was *though*, and your child said *through*, you might ask, "Did I hear an *r?*" If your child cannot decode the word after a short pause, offer the correct word to keep things moving. Have your child repeat the word back to you five times. Rereading misread words will help improve your child's ability to decode words in the future. Remember to show your child appreciation for their efforts.

Rereading sentences read correctly: After learning many words, your child will read phrases and sentences from the scriptures. When your child reads correctly but very slowly, occasionally ask your child to reread a selection. If a sentence is long, have your child go back to a certain word and reread part of the sentence. This will help improve your child's comprehension and fluency.

Rereading sentences misread: As your child's scripture reading becomes more fluent, a word may be misread, inserted, or even omitted when a phrase or sentence is read quickly. Let your child finish reading the sentence. If it did not make sense, your child may correct the phrase automatically. If your child starts to read the next sentence, ask your child to wait a moment.

If a misread sentence made sense, you might say, "That was close, but look again." If the sentence did not make sense, repeat the phrase as you heard it. This prompts your child to go back and check the sentence. If needed, point to the misread word and ask your child to tell it to you. If the word is again misread, point to the misread letter. If needed, ask your child to tell you its sound. After a short pause you may need to provide the correct sound. Now have your child try to read the word again. Tell your child the word if it is difficult.

Finally, ask your child to read the sentence or phrase once more. Offer to read it to your child if it is still difficult. Rereading will help improve your child's comprehension and fluency. Be sure to show appreciation for your child's efforts.

Rereading automatically: Without being prompted, your child may reread words or sentences read correctly, but slowly. Your child may also instinctively correct misread words. If your child automatically goes back and corrects a word in a sentence, compliment them at that time, and do not ask for the sentence to be reread. Asking your child to repeat only the sentences they do not correct will encourage self-correction. Rereading is a habit possessed by good readers. The purpose of rereading is to help prepare your child to read silently.

A Few Minutes Each Day

The previous methods are to assist you in helping your child develop the habit of daily scripture reading, while teaching them reading and writing skills. Use these methods to spend a small amount of time each day reading together. Keep it short and keep it fun. Read a storybook together in the morning or at night. Sometime during the day, practice a letter. If you see your child needs a break, practice a word at another time. You may need to offer your child a small incentive or make a deal with them to encourage cooperation.

Give your child choices whenever you can. Would he rather read before watching TV or before snack time? Does he want to sit on your lap or next to you at the table? Does he want to read a story first or practice with the flashcards? These kinds of questions show that you respect your child's opinion and individuality. Letting your child make choices also helps them develop independent thinking and feel responsible for their decisions. Make sure your child sticks to their decision. (Remind them they can choose differently *next* time.) This way, your child will gain the satisfaction that comes from completing a task.

Celebrate each little success your child makes. Encourage your child by showing appreciation for their efforts each step of the way. Give praise often. A child may need a positive word, a simple nod, or a gentle squeeze after *every* word that is read correctly. Be sure to give lots of love.

The methods described here promote learning through the use of the various senses. When information is impressed upon the mind in various ways, it increases the likelihood that it will be remembered. Your child will learn letters, numbers, and words through seeing, hearing, speaking, and touching. Your child will see these letters on flashcards, look for them in the scriptures, listen to them spoken, repeat them back, touch them on flashcards, and write them down. This also complements the individual learning styles of various children.

The repetition used by this program also sets your child up for success. Your child practices letters (numbers or words) using flashcards, and looks for them again in the scriptures. This routine is only repeated until your child can remember them. Then, after your child has learned just 50 words, your child will read these words when starting the Book of Mormon from the beginning. This repetition provides a positive reading experience to help your child feel successful.

The flashcards with words on them are not printed in the same font as the letter flashcards because the word flashcards use the same font as the Book of Mormon. Because of this you may need to help your child recognize the letters *a*, *g*, and *q*. Also, there are serifs (little tick marks) at the bottom of *f, h, i, l, m, n, p,* and *r*, and the *t* has a curl. It is all right if your child copies this lettering when practicing words using these flashcards. However, make sure your child copies the primer font when practicing letters. This is because the letter flashcards will teach your child to write as required for school.

On page 127 is a handy chart depicting the order you will use to teach the top 50 words from the Book of Mormon. During this process, let your child use his or her own scriptures to circle letters and numbers and to underline words. Your child's book will become special to them as they use it every day. Be sure your child sees that you enjoy reading your scriptures and marking in them too.

If you are consistent, your child will learn to become a competent reader, prepared for all the choices life brings their way. Your child will become more familiar with the various lessons contained in the scriptures, while developing a daily habit of reading them. Both of you will find that many blessings come from daily scripture reading!

3 Program Background

Developing the Habit

My husband and I have made a habit of family scripture reading. We have used a variety of methods and read together as a family even when it didn't seem like anyone was paying any attention. Little by little, we watched as our children's attention span grew and their reading abilities improved. We were consistent because we wanted to teach our children the importance of scripture reading.

We were also successful at encouraging our children to read the scriptures each day on their own. When the older children were in elementary school, they could earn a dollar a week (or 20 cents a day) for reading one chapter of the Book of Mormon for five days. By the time our younger children began to read, this became 15 cents a day, seven days a week.

The children used a homemade "point chart" to keep track of their earnings so that no money changed hands. They recorded various tasks by its initial, each initial worth five cents. Some tasks received several initials. The children learned how to add up these points and often crossed them off after a trip to the store. The points could also buy a small candy bar or a soda pop from our basement.

When the older children started junior high school, it was important for them to have name-brand tennis shoes. We then changed our incentive and took them shopping when they were finished reading the Book of Mormon. Their rate of reading was to be no more than one chapter per day, and no points were given. One daughter chose a comparable amount to be spent on school clothes. Normally, shopping for school clothes took place when an individual article was needed, or when other avenues had run out: hand-me-downs, second-hand stores, or asking Grandma!

When our teenagers studied the New Testament or the Doctrine and Covenants in seminary, we kept their "shoes" incentive the same, even though those books are shorter. In seminary they were encouraged to read their scriptures every day. Their example humbled me, and I learned to read my scriptures on the weekends as well. As our children have served missions, they have expressed gratitude to us for giving them this good habit.

Learning to Read the Scriptures

It was a struggle for me to learn to make a habit of daily personal scripture reading. But now I love to read the scriptures. I think it would have been easier for me to make a habit of it if I had started reading the scriptures when I was younger. This encouraged me to use the Book of Mormon to teach our youngest child to read.

When our first child, Levi, was about two years old, I read about a program to teach a baby to read. The flashcards I made came in handy later on, but it was a rather short-lived experiment. By the time he was four and a half, he was joined by a brother, Sean, and two sisters, Brit and Emma. Those were exciting but tiring times!

When the children entered school, I found it difficult to keep up with their schoolwork. I hadn't learned how simple it could be and what little time it would take to teach a preschooler to read using the scriptures. I wish I had taught the older children to read at a younger age.

By the time our fifth and sixth children, Hope and Ford, started school, there were no more new babies. So, during the day

I spent one-on-one time with Cade, our youngest. For various reasons, he was the only one of our children who missed an opportunity to attend preschool. Because of this I am glad I was prompted to teach him to read—and thankful I discovered the scriptures to be a useful tool to do so. Cade became an excellent reader, and he developed the habit of daily scripture reading early in his life.

Letters and Numbers

When Ford was in first grade he brought home little reading books to practice and return. Cade liked to watch us read together. One day when we were done with the book, Cade wanted a turn too. So, during the year prior to his starting kindergarten, I decided to help him learn to read.

The first thing I did was have Cade pretend to read. Choosing an easy book, I read a sentence to him while pointing to each word. Then I asked him to repeat the sentence with me slowly, while I pointed to the words again. We repeated this on each page.

To help him learn what a word was, I soon asked him to point to them the first time through. I read them as slowly as he pointed to them. Sometimes he wanted to point to the words when he read them back with me. I often had to remind him to slow down, because his finger would get to the end of a sentence before we were done saying the words! Eventually he could stay on the right word without me reading it with him. When he got really good at mimicking me, I read two sentences to him before he read them back.

After a few weeks, I found a workbook for Cade that showed how to make letters and numbers. At first, I didn't tell him how to make the letters. I just told him to copy them carefully. When he was done with a page we always enjoyed taking turns picking out his nicest creations. After a while I gradually gave him more instructions, explaining that he should make the letters by starting at the top. Later on, I told him to make sure the letters "kiss the line!"

The next thing I did was to teach Cade the names of the letters. I typed up the alphabet in a large font on our computer. I printed out a sheet of paper with each lowercase and matching uppercase letter right next to each other. Each morning we went over the sheet.

As I pointed to a letter, I paused for a few seconds to see if he remembered it. If he didn't, I told him its name. Singing the alphabet song, and going slow on the "l-m-n-o-p" part, helped him learn the names of the letters. I crossed off the letters that he could remember and he got to skip them after that. He liked getting them crossed off, and it helped him see his progress. I made up a new page when all the letters were crossed off.

The second sheet had the numbers from 0 through 11 printed on it. We reviewed it each morning, crossing off the numbers he remembered. When they were all crossed off, I wanted him to review the letters again. This time I arranged the alphabet into rows of letters with similar shapes. I placed each uppercase letter right below its matching lowercase letter. If a whole page of letters seemed too much for him to do in one sitting, I folded the sheet in half.

After reviewing the letters, I made up a second sheet of numbers, counting by tens through 100. On Cade's third alphabet sheet, I left the letters in rows of similar shapes, but this time the matching lowercase and uppercase letters were not right next to each other.

Next, I made up a third page of numbers, counting by fives through 95. I arranged them so the numbers ending in fives were all lined up in columns, next to a column of the numbers ending in zeros.

Cade's final alphabet sheet had all the letters in random order, and his last number sheet was from 1 through 50. Finally, he passed off a sheet with a combination of both letters and numbers.

At first, Cade liked the extra attention these daily lessons gave him. But there were also times when he needed some persuasion. He liked learning new things, but he was also the most strong-willed of our children. Sometimes I had to make deals with him. If there was something fun he wanted to do, I told him he needed to do his "homework" first.

Adding Words

One spring day while Cade was learning the names of letters and numbers, our elementary school held a Getting to Know You Day for the following year's kindergarten children. I asked Cade's future teacher if she had a list of beginning words that I could start teaching him. She gave me a sheet of cardstock that had twelve "sight" words printed on each side. She told me I could cut it apart to use as flashcards. These words could not be sounded out and needed to be memorized. I decided I would teach Cade these words one at a time.

The first flashcard I showed Cade had the word *a* on it. I told him the word, and then I had him say it back to me ten times while he counted on his fingers. I challenged him to see if he could remember the word by the next morning. Later that day I asked him a few times if he still remembered the word, and I reminded him if he didn't. I brought out a new flashcard when he could remember his word the next day.

Each morning Cade completed a page in his writing workbook, and we read a storybook together. We also practiced an alphabet or number sheet and one word flashcard. Last, we reviewed the flashcards he already knew. As the flashcard pile grew, I removed the words he was really good at reading. Cade learned little by little, and we didn't spend a lot of time each day. Sometimes we brought the flashcards along in the car to practice. Other days we forgot to practice at all, especially on the weekends, but mostly we were consistent.

When Cade had finished all the sheets I made up and knew the names of the letters, I taught him the sounds they make. I found a set of small plastic tiles at the store. Half of them had letters, and the other half had pictures that matched their sounds. Each morning we matched the letters to the pictures and repeated their sounds. If Cade could remember any new sounds that day, I let him put those tiles in a separate bag. Occasionally we reviewed them.

Since the sounds of some letters don't seem to make sense, I taught Cade some tricks. One way I helped him remember the sound of a *w* was to tell him to call it a *wubble-u*. He also liked the way I taught him the short *u* sound—by the grunt I made while pretending to punch myself in the stomach. Besides the one picture that came with each tile, I taught Cade both of the sounds for *c* and *g* and both the short and long vowel sounds.

After Cade could match up all the tiles, we practiced with another set of tiles that was designed for building words. Each of these tiles had a combination of letters (blends and digraphs) that together made a brand-new sound. To remind him of the sound for *th*, I showed him my thumb; to teach him the sound for *sh*, I brought my finger to my lips.

The Book of Mormon

When I started teaching Cade the sight words with the flashcards, I also started reading my scriptures in the morning, rather than at night when I was tired. Cade saw me reading one morning and got out his copy of the Book of Mormon that he took to church. Since I use colored pencils when I read, he got some out too. He sat down next to me at the kitchen table and mimicked me by underlining words on various pages in his scriptures. I felt inspired to get out the flashcard he was practicing that day.

I placed the flashcard in front of him and asked him to find the word in his scriptures. He found one right away! Since that was so easy for him, I decided to ask him to find four more. I had him show me the word each time he found one, and read it aloud. When he was done, I told him he had just read his scriptures for the very first time! I decided to teach Cade his sight words this way each morning while I read my scriptures.

At the time I remember thinking about the early American settlers and those in Europe who lived during the reformation. The invention of the printing press brought the Bible to the common people. They wanted to be able to read it for themselves, and many times it was the only book a family could afford. It seemed to me that the family Bible would have been what they used to teach their children to read.

It was probably not a new idea to use the scriptures as Cade's primer. However, I chose to use the Book of Mormon instead. That book has always been special to me, and I was reading it at the time. Also, Cade had his own copy. Besides that, the language of the Book of Mormon seemed to me to be easier to read than the Bible.

Each morning I sat on the couch, put Cade on my lap, and helped him review his flashcards. I gave him a new flashcard if he remembered yesterday's word. I told him what the word was and asked him to repeat it back to me ten times. After that we moved to the kitchen and sat side by side at the table. While I read my scriptures, Cade read his scriptures. Each day he used his flashcard to look for his word five times. When he found his word, I told him to underline it, and he read it to me. He liked keeping track of how many times he found a word by making little marks at the top of his page. Cade often forgot his word while he was looking for it. If he did, I had him look at the flashcard again and repeat it to me five more times.

Sometimes Cade didn't feel like looking for his words. And sometimes a word was really hard to find. When this happened, I told him to look just a little bit longer—while I read just three verses in my scriptures. Giving him a time limit helped him agree to look harder and he often found the word.

When Cade still needed help to find a word, I looked through a few of his pages for him. When I found the word, I told him which verse number to look at. This helped him review his numbers and to learn what a verse was. If he couldn't find it, I told him which page, or column, the number was on. If needed, I then pointed to the verse.

The Top 50 Words

As we progressed, I wondered if Cade's flashcard words were also some of the most common words used in the Book of Mormon. I had an old DOS computer edition of the scriptures (Gospel Infobase Library, 1992, Runtime 2.2, Folio Corporation).

The search menu in this particular program listed every word used in the standard works. By highlighting a word and clicking "enter" on the keyboard, I could see how many times that word was used in the Book of Mormon.

Years before I had used this program to make up a family game. To make the game, I had wanted to find the most commonly used words in the Book of Mormon. I had spent about a month going through the entire list of words in the program. Each day I had looked through all the words beginning with one of the letters of the alphabet. Of the thousands of words listed, I looked up the words that seemed to be the most likely candidates. I had written down all the words I could find that were used more than fifty times. I put them in order and had a list of more than 300 words.

Although much time had passed, I felt inspired to locate my list of words from the Book of Mormon. Using the top fifty most popular words, I made some more flashcards for Cade. Sixteen of his sight words were in the top fifty, so the twenty-four cards grew to fifty-eight. The shorter words were usually the easiest for Cade to learn, but the more popular words in the scriptures were the easiest for us to find. I used a combination of these two factors when deciding on the order to teach Cade the words.

After Cade learned the sounds that letters make, he slowed down a little when we reviewed his flashcards. Instead of reciting them from memory, he began to sound out the words. This often enabled him to figure out his new flashcard on his own. Sometimes he got a word the first time I showed him the card. When this happened, I got out the next card.

When a word wouldn't sound out, it helped to have Cade repeat the word both the way it looked and the correct way. For example, he might say, "p-ee-oo-pl-ee, *p-ee-pl*" or "w-at, *w-u-t*." He thought that was funny too! At his age I decided not to explain a lot of special rules to him. I often told him to just try another sound for a particular letter. If a word still wouldn't sound out, then I had him memorize it.

Reading Alternately

After many slow-going months, our small daily habits paid off. Cade learned all twenty-four sight words and the thirty-four additional words from the Book of Mormon. He was halfway through kindergarten and also knew all the sounds the letters made. Since he knew many words and could sound out many others, I was prompted to put away the flashcards. I decided he was ready to read the Book of Mormon from the beginning!

I opened up Cade's book and pointed to the words *Chapter 1*. I showed him where the first two verses were by circling their numbers. Then, I asked him to underline all the words he knew in those two verses. After he did, we both read together, taking turns. He read the words he knew, and I read the ones he didn't. After we had finished just those two verses, Cade's scripture reading was done for the day!

Circling the verse numbers helped us keep track of where we were reading each day. Cade was soon good at underlining all the words he knew in each verse, so I began to underline his words to save time. I did this while we read. This helped him know when it was his turn to read, and it helped him to stay on the right word.

As Cade's reading improved, I underlined other words I thought he would be able to sound out. After a while, he could follow along while I just pointed to his words with my pencil, without underlining them. When it was his turn to read, I paused and he read. We laughed when we got mixed-up and both said the word at the same time. By the end of kindergarten when Cade turned six, he could read several verses from the Book of Mormon to me each day.

Using this technique of reading alternately, Cade was also able to enjoy taking a turn during family scripture reading. We helped him keep up and follow along in his book by saying aloud each verse number before we read it. Sometimes he caught someone reading a word wrong. He loved trying to do that!

It seemed to me the top 50 words were about half the words we read in each verse. To find out for sure, I again went to the scripture program on our computer. First, I highlighted every word in each book of the Book of Mormon. Then I pasted them into our word processing program. Next (using "Find and Replace" in the "Edit" menu), I removed from the document all the numerals and the word *chapter.*

I found out that there are 267,306 words in the Book of Mormon (using "Word Count" in the "Tools" menu), not counting the chapter heading information. Then, one at a time, I removed the top 50 words (using "Find and Replace" again). This left 122,209 words. Subtracting these two totals meant the top 50 words were used 145,097 times—54 percent of the words in the Book of Mormon!

Reading Silently

When Cade could read almost every word in a column (half the page), I decided to have him start reading a whole page silently each day. I asked him to underline any words he came to that he didn't know. We went over these words together afterward. I also had him write the date (just the day) at the top of each page to mark his reading. This saved him on the days he accidentally lost his bookmark. When he was able to read a whole chapter each day, he marked his reading by circling the chapter number. If a chapter was long, he often asked if he could read half of it.

The children at our elementary school are required to read at home for at least twenty minutes each day. Individual scripture reading, and reading as a family, has helped our children accomplish this. When Cade started first grade, he no longer read his scriptures with me in the morning, as he had done while in afternoon kindergarten. He then read with his brother, Ford, as soon as they got home from school (after a snack, but before playing).

After Christmas, during Cade's first-grade year, we began studying the Book of Mormon in Sunday School and Primary. One Sunday in the spring, Cade's brother learned about Alma and Amulek in prison. I wanted their daily reading to mean more, so I had them both skip ahead to Alma and read from there on. They liked reading and learning about things they talked about in church.

About a year later, near the end of second grade, Cade was baptized. He was just about done with the last half of the Book of Mormon. There were days when he missed reading, and there were chapters that took more than a day. During the following summer, he began the Book of Mormon again. In third grade, before fall was over, he had reached Alma, where he had skipped to in first grade. In the third grade, by the age of eight and a half, Cade had read the whole Book of Mormon!

I wished I had read the Book of Mormon at Cade's age. I know he will gain more from the book each time he reads it. I know I do. I know he will grow to love his scriptures as I love mine. I am so grateful to have been able to help him become a good reader and to have helped him develop the habit of scripture reading early in his life.

Reading the scriptures daily has helped our children improve their reading skills and develop good scripture reading habits. It has helped them learn about the things that matter most and to "enjoy the words of eternal life" (Moses 6:59). I know daily personal and family scripture reading has blessed our family in many ways. The scriptures themselves ask us to read them and promise us many wonderful blessings.

I was not always consistent at reading the scriptures, but I have gained a testimony of its importance now that I have made it a habit. I have felt the guidance and inspiration of the Holy Spirit more in my life. My knowledge has grown of the love that the Father and the Son have for the world—throughout the ages—increasing my faith on life's journey. My knowledge and love for the gospel of Jesus Christ has grown also, which brings me great hope. I am happiest when I pattern my life the best that I can after the wisdom of those who have gone before me.

I know God is pleased with all of us as we read the words He has given to us through His inspired prophets. What a glorious way to bring the wonders of reading to the lives of our children! I hope this program will help you and your child love the scriptures more each day, while at the same time learn to be good readers. May God bless you both.

Author Background

As a Child

In my earliest memories I am sitting next to my grandmother and she's reading to me. Maybe that's why I have always loved books. Not only did I want to know the stories, but I also wanted to know the words that made them. I still remember playing school with my friends as a child. I remember wanting to know how to make numbers and letters, and I remember practicing them—especially cursive—since that was for *big* kids! As soon as I knew a few letters, I wrote little notes to my friends: "R U OK? I M 2."

When I was in elementary school, I wanted to be a schoolteacher. This was because of the kindness of my first-grade teacher, Mrs. Reddington. During recess, I often spent my time in the library reading books. In the fourth grade I fell in love with Johann Wyss' *The Swiss Family Robinson*. I had a book with me everywhere I went. For me there was no such thing as "nothing to do." Every spare minute was a chance to see something new without having to go anywhere!

I was totally amazed by two real families I read about: the Wilder family in *The Little House* series and the Gilbreth family in *Cheaper by the Dozen*. Their parents were so smart and taught their children everything. And they all enjoyed being together. With just one younger brother, I wished I had a big family. I dreamed of having children of my own to teach.

As a child and young adult, church leaders and teachers helped shape my feelings for the Book of Mormon. When I first read the Book of Mormon all the way through, it became special to me. This was in connection with a religion class at BYU in 1977. I remember feeling the warm influence of the spirit as I read and feeling very emotional when I finished the last page. I still feel this way when I read it. That class helped me understand the importance of reading the scriptures every day.

As a Young Mother

I attended Brigham Young University in Provo and Hawaii and changed my major a few times. Before finishing school, I met Mark, from Cache Valley, Utah. He came to my ward in California, near where he and a friend were working that summer. After a Christmas wedding, he finished college while we became parents.

Our seven children each bring joy to our family in their own unique way. Since I love reading and learning, I wanted our children to be good readers so they could be good learners. Through it all, I have found that teaching children can be very challenging!

I also love the scriptures. They have increased my love for family—my own family, the great human family, and a heavenly family. I was born into a loving family. I have loving children, friends, and neighbors. I have a Father in heaven who loves me unconditionally. He has sent the "good news" of the great plan of redemption, made possible by my eldest brother, Jesus Christ. He lived and gave His life for me, and saves me from mortality. I have been blessed with a sweet comforter, the Holy Ghost, who helps me on my journey back to my first home.

These are things worth learning and teaching! Learning the gospel (and how to live it) has made more of an impact on my life than anything else. The gospel is a map for me to follow. There is much joy in life. As my testimony grows, I gain added strength for my journey. When I am hurting, I have an eternal perspective. Learning these things is more important than learning other things. Now, what if the scriptures could be the very tools we use to learn to read?

In General Conference, April 1980, President Marion G. Romney gave a talk called "The Book of Mormon." Something he said has meant a lot to me, especially when I was a young mother:

> I feel certain that if, in our homes, parents will read from the Book of Mormon prayerfully and regularly, both by themselves and with their children, the spirit of that great book will come to permeate our homes and all who dwell therein. The spirit of reverence will increase; mutual respect and consideration for each other will grow. The spirit of contention will depart. Parents will counsel their children in greater love and wisdom. Children will be more responsive and submissive to the counsel of their parents. Righteousness will increase. Faith, hope, and charity—the pure love of Christ—will abound in our homes and lives, bringing in their wake peace, joy, and happiness.

As a young mother, the media impacted my desire to teach others to read. During the last half of the 1980s, Barbara Bush led a national movement promoting family literacy. Television stations sponsored a campaign called Project Literacy US (PLUS). This included a made-for-TV movie called *Bluffing It* (1987), which touched me deeply. Dennis Weaver portrayed the trials of a father who lived a life of deception because he couldn't read. Public Service Announcements also ran on television, encouraging people in the community to volunteer as reading tutors. Through this media campaign I determined (when my children were older) that I would get involved in helping others learn to do one of my favorite things—read.

In October General Conference 1988, President Ezra Taft Benson said, "I challenge the homes of Israel to display on their walls great quotations and scenes from the Book of Mormon" ("Flooding the Earth with the Book of Mormon," *Ensign*, November 1988). This inspired a calligraphy project for the sisters in our ward. We choose a favorite verse from the Book of Mormon and framed it. Mine still hangs on our wall: "May God the Father . . . bless [us] forever, through faith on . . . Jesus Christ" (Mormon 9:37).

Around that same time I spent hours going over a word list in the scripture program on our computer. I found the top fifty most commonly used words in the Book of Mormon. I wrote them on stickers and put them in egg carton flats. Our young children, who could only read a few words, could play marshmallow Bingo during family scripture reading. I have given this list to many friends who have children.

Volunteering

Over a decade later, the year before our youngest child was to start kindergarten, he wanted me to help him practice his older brother's first-grade readers with him. Soon afterward, I was inspired to teach him the top fifty words from the Book of Mormon. Because of the success we had, I began to write down the methods we used so I would remember them. This way, my children would know how to use these words to teach their children. As I began writing, I realized I should share this program with other parents.

In 2002, when our youngest child entered kindergarten, I wanted to get involved in community service. His teacher needed several parents one day a week, so I volunteered. A month or two later I found notices in the newspaper about two other opportunities. One article was looking for volunteers to teach computer classes at the senior center. The other article offered a series of classes to train tutors for the county literacy program. (This was the program I had decided in the late '80s that I would eventually get involved in.) I volunteered to teach word processing and signed up for the tutoring classes.

That Christmas our son's kindergarten teacher began sending books home for him to practice reading and bring back. These books were then read again at school and passed off. They were quite old, and the printing was sometimes hard to read. Although our son had learned many words, the books frustrated him. Each book introduced many new and complex words. I had struggled with these readers when our older children brought them home. I wanted our reading together to continue to be enjoyable.

I felt there must be a better set of beginning readers. Over a period of weeks I spoke to several people about it. I finally mentioned my dilemma to the resource teacher at our school. She said her class used a good set of readers, and she offered to let me borrow them. After our son passed off several of these books with his teacher, she began sending them home with other children. More books were ordered, and the following year they replaced the old readers.

After Christmas I began teaching word processing at the senior center one day a week. I also began tutoring reading and writing three days a week for the county literacy program. I tutored at the community high school for students who were no longer able to attend regular high school. These locations required that I make a forty-minute drive (round-trip).

Once a week I continued to help out in our son's kindergarten class. The students were divided into three learning groups, and two volunteers assisted the teacher. The groups rotated every fifteen minutes, and we helped the students with worksheets. During my visits I noticed a few of the children could really use some extra tutoring. Since our school was only a few blocks away, I told his teacher that I would be happy to come to class a few extra times each week. She was very appreciative, and I tutored a few children using the new readers. One of these children lived down our street, and I continued to tutor her throughout the summer.

The following year at Back to School Night, I offered to tutor again, this time for our son's first-grade teacher. I knew first-grade students couldn't get resource help because they weren't yet two years behind grade level. She was delighted when I told her I would like to come to school each day to tutor. Because of this commitment, I decided not to tutor at the community high school that fall. Instead, I hoped I could help a child *stay out of* community high school!

That year I also began volunteering four days a week for a program called Dialog. All the students were sorted by reading level and divided into small groups composed of various grades. These groups read together for forty-five minutes every day except Friday.

The success of this program depended upon many community volunteers. I had looked forward to helping with this program but was unable to as long as I had children at home in the morning hours.

The first Dialog group I was given consisted of six resource students from third through fifth grade. They were very active, and it was a challenge to keep their attention, but I loved every minute of it! After Christmas, I was given a group of nine students from first through third grade who read at a fifth-grade level. In the spring, I had seven students from the second and third grades, reading at a seventh-grade level. I enjoyed going over many chapter books with them.

The children I had tutored in kindergarten began to mature in first grade. That seemed to help them pay attention and learn faster. I wasn't able to help all the children I had tutored in kindergarten because there were three first-grade classes. The time I spent tutoring (and helping in Dialog) totaled more than two hours a day. Still, I worried that there were other first-grade children that needed more help!

That December I gave my resignation to the senior center. I gathered up the handouts, instruction sheets, projects, and samples I had developed (there was no manual) and put a book together to donate to the center for Christmas. A student could use this handbook as a personal guide until a new teacher was found. There were fewer class members because of the holidays, and the past year had taught me that my real love was teaching children.

When our son began second grade, I continued to tutor for the same teacher I had helped the year before. It was very satisfying to see first-grade children begin the year knowing only a handful of words, and finish the year reading a hundred or more! At first I tutored every day, but because of their progress, I tutored only three days a week after Christmas.

I also volunteered for Dialog again that year. I had two groups of eight students from fourth and fifth grade. The first group read at an eighth-grade level, and the second group at a fifth-grade level. This lasted until Christmas, when the program was phased out.

The following summer I again volunteered for the county literacy program. They had arranged with some elementary schools (not ours, however) to find students who could use summer tutoring. I chose a little boy who had just finished kindergarten but didn't know all of his letters. I tutored him two days a week for thirty minutes at the public library.

For the first several sessions, my student didn't seem very happy that his mother had signed him up for the program. I did everything I could think of to help him become involved and have an enjoyable time. I offered him choices whenever possible to make his learning more fun. I made up games with letters, and at each visit I let him choose a story for me to read to him. When I realized he had a hard time telling the difference between several colors, I adapted some of my techniques. After a while our sessions grew to an hour long, and he wanted me to come and tutor him three days a week!

The literacy program provided many teaching aids, and one of their offices was there in the library. After our lessons, I often exchanged ideas with the coordinators. I enjoyed visiting with them, and they always left me feeling good about my efforts.

I was unhappy with the phonics flashcards that I found and made my own set using photographs of real objects. I designed each card so the lowercase letter was directly above the uppercase letter. This way the cards could easily be used to build words by placing them side-by-side. I also donated a set to each of the literacy program's two offices.

At the end of the summer, I was delighted to accept a position to serve on the literacy program's advisory board. When school began in the fall, the summer tutoring program was officially over, but I continued to meet with my student each Saturday. About a month later the family moved away.

When our son began third grade, I was inspired to go to the principal (instead of a teacher) to see if any help was needed tutoring reading in first grade. The principal was very kind to allow me half an hour a day—*in each of the three classes*! I was very excited to finally be able to tutor all the first-grade students who needed my help the most!

A Teacher's Aide

That December, I was asked to fill in as a literacy substitute at the elementary school. This was a half-day position on Wednesday mornings. It required testing students from each grade in fluency, and substituting for various teachers during their weekly meetings. I continued to accept this assignment a couple of times each month for the rest of the year.

In February, a teacher's aide was needed for a program called Guided Reading (which replaced Dialog). It entailed leading two small groups of second-grade students in reading, writing, and discussing chapter books. Each group met for a half an hour, every day but Wednesday. I applied for the position and was offered it. For the remainder of that year, I limited my tutoring in first grade to four days a week instead of five.

As I tutor children of all ages and personalities, I continue to come upon new challenges. I pray regularly to have the spirit guide my efforts and have received many insights. These are faith-promoting experiences. I have incorporated each of those insights into this program.

Over the years many people have helped to bring about this program. As I continue to learn throughout my life, I am very grateful to all those who have taught me. I hope this book will help others and that I can in this small way give something back.

The profits from Barbara Bush's children's books were donated to literacy. Following her example, my royalties from the sale of this book will benefit education, through the Perpetual Education Fund, a division of LDS Philanthropies, of The Church of Jesus Christ of Latter-day Saints. I love these words from the mission statement of the Barbara Bush Foundation for Family Literacy: "To establish literacy as a value in every family in America, by helping every family in the nation understand that the home is the child's first school, that the parent is the child's first teacher, and that reading is the child's first subject."

5 Program References

Top 50 References

Below are over fifty references for each of the top fifty words in the Book of Mormon. Some words are easier to find in certain areas of the Book of Mormon, so be sure to browse.

1. I

1 Nephi 1:1(3), 2, 3(4), 13, 16(2), 17(5), 18, 20
1 Nephi 2:1, 16(4), 17, 18, 20, 23
1 Nephi 3:5(2), 7(3), 8–10, 13, 15, 21
1 Nephi 4:1, 4, 5(2), 6(2), 7(3), 8(2), 9(3), 10(6), 11, 14(2), 15, 16, 17(2), 18(2)

2. a

1 Nephi 5:2, 4(2), 5, 8(2), 12, 14(2), 16
1 Nephi 8:2(2), 4, 5(2), 7, 9, 10, 13–15, 19, 20(3), 23, 26, 36, 37
1 Nephi 9:1(2), 2(2), 3, 5, 6
1 Nephi 10:4(3), 5, 6(2), 7, 16, 17
1 Nephi 11:6, 7(2), 8, 11(3), 13, 15, 19, 20, 25(2), 27, 35

3. of

1 Nephi 6:1(2), 2, 3(4), 4(4), 5, 6(2)

1 Nephi 7:1(2), 2, 4(3), 5(2), 6(3), 7–10, 11(2), 12, 13(4), 14(3), 15, 17, 19(4), 20(2), 21, 22(3)

4. to

1 Nephi 12:1(4), 2, 3, 4(6), 5(4), 6(2), 7, 8, 9(6), 10(2), 11(3), 12–14, 15(2), 16(3), 17(4), 18(7)

5. and

1 Nephi 13:1(4), 2(3), 3(2), 4, 5(5), 6(3), 7(7), 8(8), 9(2), 10(3), 11, 12(5), 13(2), 14(4), 15(6)

6. the

1 Nephi 14:1(3), 2(5), 3(7), 4(3), 5(5), 6(2), 7(11), 8(4), 9(2), 10(11), 11(3), 12(13)

7. in

1 Nephi 15:1, 3, 11(2), 12, 13(4), 16, 18(2), 19, 21, 25, 27, 31, 32, 33(2), 35
1 Nephi 16:5, 6(2), 10, 14(4), 16, 20, 24, 28, 33, 34, 35(3)
1 Nephi 17:1(3), 2–4, 7, 12–14, 19(2), 20(2), 21

8. it

1 Nephi 18:1, 2(2), 4(2), 5, 6, 8, 11(2), 12, 15, 20, 21(4), 22, 23(2), 24(2), 25
1 Nephi 19:1, 6(2), 9(3), 19, 21, 22(2), 23
1 Nephi 22:1, 3, 6–9, 14, 17(2), 18(3), 20, 22, 28, 31

9. that

1 Nephi 20:4, 6, 8(2), 9, 16, 18
1 Nephi 21:1(3), 5(2), 6(2), 7, 9(2), 10, 14, 15, 17, 19, 20, 23(2), 25, 26(2)
2 Nephi 1:1–4, 6, 7, 8(2), 9(3), 10(3), 12(2), 13(2), 16–18, 19(2), 20, 21(4)

10. they

2 Nephi 2:4, 5(3), 8–10, 19, 20, 21(2), 22(3), 23(4), 25, 26(2), 27

2 Nephi 5:2, 3, 4(2), 6, 16, 18(2), 19, 20(3), 21(4), 22(2), 23, 24, 25(3), 26, 32, 33

2 Nephi 6:4, 5(2), 6, 7(2), 9(2), 10(2), 11(4)

11. unto

2 Nephi 3:1, 2, 4, 5(5), 6, 7(3), 8, 9(2), 11(2), 12, 13, 15(2), 16, 17(3), 18(4), 19(2), 20, 21(3), 23, 24(3), 25(2)

2 Nephi 4:3(2), 7(2), 9(3), 10(2), 11(5), 12, 14(2)

12. he

2 Nephi 8:3(2), 9, 10, 12(2), 13, 14(2)

2 Nephi 9:1, 2, 5(2), 17, 19, 20(2), 21(3), 22, 25, 34, 35, 41(2), 42(3), 44, 50, 53(2)

2 Nephi 16:2(3), 6, 7, 9, 11

2 Nephi 20:7, 8, 13, 16, 24, 26, 28(3), 32(2), 34

13. be

2 Nephi 10:2–4(2), 5, 6(2), 7, 8(2), 9, 10(2), 11(2), 14(2), 15, 18(2), 19, 21, 25

2 Nephi 12:2(2), 6, 11(3), 12, 17(3), 22

2 Nephi 15:5(2), 6, 8(2), 9, 15(3), 16(2), 24, 26, 27(2), 28(2)

14. for

2 Nephi 11:1, 2(3), 4(2), 7(2), 8

2 Nephi 17:4(2), 6, 8, 13, 16, 18(2), 22(2), 23, 25

2 Nephi 18:4, 10, 11, 14(4), 17, 18(2), 19

2 Nephi 19:4–6, 12, 13, 16, 17(2), 18, 21

2 Nephi 21:1, 2, 9(2), 13, 21(2), 22, 23, 27, 29, 31

15. not

2 Nephi 23:3, 10(2), 17, 18, 22
2 Nephi 25:1, 2, 4, 6(2), 8, 16, 18(2), 27–29
2 Nephi 27:4(2), 8, 10, 15, 16, 19(3), 20–23, 27, 33
Jacob 4:3, 4, 8–10, 12(2), 13(2), 14, 18
Jacob 7:5, 7, 9, 11, 12, 14(2)
Jarom 1:2(2), 3, 4(2), 5, 9, 10, 14

16. his

2 Nephi 30:2, 8(2), 9(2), 10, 11(2), 14
Jacob 1:3(2), 6, 7(2), 8(2), 9, 10, 11(2), 15
Jacob 5:3–5, 7, 11, 14(2), 15, 16, 21, 23, 24, 29, 34, 35, 38,
    48, 70, 75(3)
Jacob 6:2(4), 3–6

17. all

2 Nephi 26:4, 6, 8, 13, 15, 22, 24, 25, 27(2), 28, 30, 33(2)
2 Nephi 28:8, 11, 14, 15(2), 18, 21(2), 23, 25, 28, 32
2 Nephi 33:1, 10(2), 12, 13(2)
Mosiah 1:1(3), 2, 4, 9, 10(2), 11, 15, 18
Mosiah 2:1(2), 4, 7–9, 11(2), 13, 14, 20–22

18. Alma

Mosiah 23:1, 6, 15, 16, 26, 27, 29, 35, 36, 37(2)
Mosiah 24:8, 9, 12, 15, 17, 18, 20(2), 21, 23
Mosiah 25:6, 10, 14, 15, 17, 18(2), 19, 21
Mosiah 26:7–10, 12, 13, 15, 33, 34, 37, 38
Mosiah 27:1(2), 8(2), 13, 14, 16–19, 22, 23, 32(2)

19. Nephi

Helaman 5:1, 4, 14, 16, 18, 20(2), 23(2), 26, 36, 37, 44
Helaman 8:1, 3(2), 7, 10, 22
Helaman 9:1, 4, 5, 8, 11, 14, 15, 16(2), 18, 19, 21, 27, 36–40
Helaman 10:1, 2, 4, 6, 12–15, 19
Helaman 11:1, 3, 5(2), 7, 8, 9(2)

20. them

2 Nephi 29:1, 4, 5(3), 11, 14
Jacob 3:5, 6(2), 8, 9(2), 10, 12(3)
Enos 1:9, 10, 14, 16, 18, 20, 23(5)
Jarom 1:3(2), 7, 11(2), 12(2), 14
Omni 1:3, 6(2), 7(2), 9, 16, 17(3), 21, 22, 24(2), 28, 30(2)

21. came

Mosiah 7:1–3, 5, 8, 9, 14, 17, 18
Mosiah 10:1, 3, 6, 8(2), 9, 10(2), 20, 21
Mosiah 11:1, 8, 12–18, 20, 26
Mosiah 18:1, 4, 6–8, 12, 14, 17, 18, 30(2), 32, 34
Mosiah 19:1, 5, 10, 11, 13, 14, 18(2), 22, 24, 25, 27

22. pass

Words of Mormon 1:4, 10, 13–16
Mosiah 12:1–4, 6, 8, 9, 17, 18, 20, 31
Mosiah 20:2, 6, 9–12, 24, 25(2)
Mosiah 22:1–3, 6, 7(2), 9, 11, 14, 15
Alma 2:1, 5, 7, 9, 14, 15, 19, 20, 23, 26, 29, 30, 35, 38

23. were

Mosiah 9:2, 3(3), 4, 12(2), 14, 15, 17, 19
Mosiah 16:4(2), 12(3)
Mosiah 21:5, 10–12, 21, 24(2), 25, 29, 33, 34, 35(2)
Mosiah 28:3, 4, 11(3), 12, 13, 14(2), 17(3), 18
Mosiah 29:3, 4(2), 13, 18, 19, 25, 36, 37, 39, 44

24. God

2 Nephi 7:4, 5, 7, 9
2 Nephi 31:3(2), 4–6, 13, 16, 20, 21(2)
Mosiah 3:2, 8, 11–14, 19, 21(2), 22(2), 23, 26
Mosiah 4:2, 5, 6, 9, 10, 11(2), 12, 14, 18, 19, 21, 22, 26, 30
Mosiah 5:3, 5(2), 8–10, 12, 15(2)

25. had

Mosiah 6:1, 2(2), 3(5), 7
Mosiah 8:1–4, 6, 8, 9, 19
Alma 1:1(2), 3, 4(2), 10, 15, 19, 26, 27, 30, 33
Alma 8:1(2), 4, 6, 8, 9, 13, 18, 23, 26, 31, 32
Alma 12:1(3), 7(2), 18, 19, 23, 25, 28(2), 30

26. Lord

2 Nephi 13:1(2), 8, 13–16, 17(2), 18
2 Nephi 14:2, 4, 5
2 Nephi 22:1, 2, 4, 5
Jacob 2:4, 11, 23–27, 28(2), 29–31, 32(2), 33
Mosiah 13:3, 5(2), 13, 15(2), 18, 19(2), 20, 26, 29
Mosiah 15:11(2), 18, 24(2), 26, 27(2), 28, 29(2), 30, 31

27. which

Alma 3:5(2), 6(2), 8, 11(2), 12, 14, 20, 26
Alma 6:1, 7(3), 8(4)
Alma 7:5(2), 6–13, 15(2), 16, 17(2), 19, 20(3), 21, 22, 26(2)
Alma 10:1, 2(2), 6, 11, 12(2), 13, 16, 24, 25

28. their

Alma 13:3, 4(4), 5(2), 10(2), 11, 12(2), 16
Alma 14:2(2), 3, 5, 8(2), 11, 14, 15, 20(2), 21, 22, 23(2), 25, 27, 28(2)
Alma 15:2(2), 15(2), 17(2)
Alma 16:5, 7, 8(3), 9, 11(2), 13(3), 14, 16, 17

29. shall

Mosiah 14:2(2), 8, 10(3), 11(4), 12
Alma 9:2, 13(3), 15, 18(5), 19, 24, 26(2), 28(3)
Alma 11:21(2), 22, 32, 34(2), 35(2), 36, 40(3), 41, 42(2), 43(3), 44(4)

30. did

Alma 17:2, 5, 7, 10, 15, 18, 32(3), 34, 35(2), 36, 37
Alma 19:3, 6, 16, 33(2), 34, 35(3), 36(2)
Alma 21:3, 8, 12, 17, 21(3), 23(3)
Alma 23:6, 7(2), 14, 15, 18(2)
Alma 25:1, 13, 14(3), 15(2), 16(3), 17

31. my

Alma 5:3, 6, 8, 11(2), 14, 22, 24, 26, 43(2), 49, 50, 53, 57, 58(2)
Alma 20:3, 9(2), 19, 22, 24, 26(2), 27
Alma 24:7(2), 8, 9, 10(2), 11, 12, 16
Alma 26:1(2), 11(5), 12(2), 20, 21, 23, 24, 26, 35(2), 36(7), 37(4)

32. ye

2 Nephi 32:1(4), 2(4), 3, 4(4), 5(2), 6, 8(4), 9(3)
Alma 30:8(2), 13(3), 14(2), 15(4), 16(2), 22(3), 24(3), 25, 26(3), 27(3), 39, 40(2), 41(2)

33. is

Alma 18:2(2), 3(2), 4(2), 8, 9, 11, 13, 16(2), 17(2), 22, 24, 26, 28(2), 30, 31, 34, 39
Alma 32:12(3), 13, 16(2), 18, 19, 20(2), 21–24, 26(2), 28(2), 30(2), 31, 32(3), 33, 34(3)

34. now

Alma 22:1, 3, 5, 7, 8, 18, 20–24, 28, 32, 34, 35
Alma 29:1, 3, 4, 13, 17–20, 24, 25
Alma 31:1, 3–5, 7, 8, 12, 19, 21–24, 36, 38
Alma 37:1, 5, 6, 8, 10, 11, 14, 15, 19, 21, 24, 26, 27, 32, 38, 43(2), 45, 47

35. was

Alma 28:2, 3, 4(2), 5, 6
Alma 36:2, 10, 11, 12(2), 13, 16, 17(2), 19, 20(2), 21
Alma 42:4, 6, 8, 9, 12, 16(2), 17(2), 18–21
Alma 43:5, 9, 16, 17(2), 20(2), 27(2), 29, 30, 33, 34, 35(3), 37(2), 38, 44, 46

36. yea

Alma 4:2, 4(2), 7(2), 9, 12
Alma 33:4, 5, 8, 9, 10(2), 19
Alma 34:2–4, 9(2), 10, 13, 14, 18–23, 27, 31, 32, 36, 39
Alma 44:2, 4–7, 17, 18(2), 21
Alma 45:1, 3, 5, 7, 9, 11(2), 12(3), 16, 17, 21, 22

37. have

Alma 38:2(2), 3, 6, 7, 9, 10, 13
Alma 41:1(3), 5, 9, 11, 14(4)
Alma 54:5(2), 7, 8(2), 9, 13(2), 16, 19, 21, 22(2)
Alma 60:1, 2(2), 3, 5(2), 8(6), 9(3), 10(2), 11(2), 12(4)

38. with

Alma 47:1(2), 6, 8, 10, 12, 13(2), 14, 15(2), 20, 21, 23, 31–34, 36
Alma 49:2(2), 6(3), 13, 16, 17, 20, 21(2), 22, 26, 27
Alma 52:2, 15, 17, 18, 20(2), 24(2), 26(2), 28, 29, 33, 35, 36(2), 39

39. this

Alma 27:3, 4(2), 5, 12(5), 16, 18(2), 22, 23(2), 24, 25
Alma 39:2–4, 6, 9, 14, 16(2), 17(2), 18, 19
Alma 40:2(2), 4, 5, 7, 8, 9(2), 11, 13, 14(2), 15(2), 17(3), 21, 22, 24
Alma 53:2, 5(2), 12, 15(2), 16, 18–20

40. by

Alma 50:1, 9, 11, 13(2), 15, 22, 25, 26, 28, 34(3), 35(3), 38
Alma 51:6–8, 11, 19–22, 25, 26, 27(2), 29, 31(2), 32, 33(2)
Alma 58:1, 6, 8, 9, 13, 14, 19(2), 20(2), 23, 24, 26, 28, 31(2), 39

41. people

Alma 35:4, 5(2), 6, 8(3), 9–13, 15(3)
Alma 46:4, 5, 7, 10, 19, 21, 28, 29(3), 30, 34
Alma 48:1, 2, 4, 7, 12(2), 13, 16, 19, 20
Alma 59:1, 2, 5, 7–9, 11, 12
Alma 63:1, 7, 9, 10, 15, 16

42. behold

Alma 55:2, 3(2), 18, 19, 22, 24, 31, 33
Alma 57:6, 8, 14, 17(3), 19, 20, 22, 28, 30, 31(2), 34(2), 35(2)
Alma 60:1, 2(2), 3–6, 9, 10, 11(2), 12–14, 17, 23(2), 24, 25, 27–29, 30(2), 31–34, 35(2), 36

43. who

Helaman 1:2(2), 3(2), 4, 9, 12, 16, 20, 21, 25, 30, 33
Helaman 2:1, 2, 3(2), 4, 5, 8
Helaman 3:3, 5–7, 9, 12, 23, 24, 27, 28(2), 33
Helaman 6:2, 11, 15, 18, 19, 22(3), 24, 26, 27, 28(4), 29, 30
Helaman 12:1, 6, 18, 23, 25(2), 26

44. but

Helaman 16:2(2), 6, 12, 13, 16, 20(3)
3 Nephi 12:13(2), 15, 17, 18, 22, 28, 33, 34, 37, 39(2), 44
3 Nephi 13:1, 3, 6, 7, 12, 15, 17, 18, 20, 23, 33
3 Nephi 18:13(2), 22, 23, 25, 30–32, 37
3 Nephi 28:7, 8, 16, 18, 20, 25, 26, 37, 39, 40

45. also

3 Nephi 2:1, 4(3), 5, 10(2), 12
4 Nephi 1:1(2), 4, 6(2), 14(2), 19, 21(3), 33, 41, 43
Mormon 3:10, 17, 19(2), 21(2)
Mormon 5:4, 9(3), 10, 15, 21
Mormon 7:5, 8, 9(2), 10
Ether 2:1, 2(2), 3, 16, 19, 20, 24
Ether 6:4, 6, 7, 15–17, 29, 30

46. upon

Helaman 7:6, 10(2), 11, 14, 15, 21
Helaman 13:4, 5, 17(2), 20(2), 21, 23(2), 32
Helaman 14:11, 18, 20–22, 28, 29(2)
3 Nephi 3:3, 6, 8, 16, 20(2), 24
3 Nephi 4:6(2), 7, 10, 18, 21, 22, 28(2)
3 Nephi 8:10, 18(2), 19, 20, 22, 23
3 Nephi 14:24, 25(2), 26, 27

47. him

3 Nephi 17:5(2), 9, 10, 12(2), 15, 17
3 Nephi 29:5(2), 6, 7
Ether 3:7, 9, 11, 13, 18(2), 20, 26(6), 27, 28
Ether 7:4, 5, 9, 10, 13, 17, 18(3), 22
Ether 8:3, 5, 6(3), 9, 10(3), 11(2), 12, 14, 22

48. are

Alma 61:1, 3(3), 6, 7
Helaman 15:2, 3, 5, 6(3), 7(3), 8, 10
3 Nephi 10:4(2), 14, 16, 17(2)
3 Nephi 15:7, 12(3), 17, 21(2), 24(2)
3 Nephi 16:1, 2, 6, 8(2), 9(2), 14
3 Nephi 24:1, 6, 7, 9, 15(2)
3 Nephi 27:3, 8, 9, 11, 12, 22, 23, 26, 30, 31(2), 32

49. land

Alma 62:3, 4, 6(3), 7, 11–13, 14(2), 15, 18, 25, 30(2), 32–34,
    38, 42, 46, 48(2), 51
Helaman 4:2, 5(3), 6, 8, 9, 12
3 Nephi 1:1–3, 7, 17(2), 23, 27, 28
3 Nephi 6:2(2), 3(2), 4–6, 8(2), 11, 14(2)

50. should

Alma 56:5, 8(2), 21, 23, 24(2), 30, 37, 39, 40(2), 43, 46(2)
3 Nephi 19:3, 5, 6(2), 9, 16(2), 17, 24
3 Nephi 23:6, 9(5), 13, 14
3 Nephi 26:2(2), 3(5), 9, 13, 16
3 Nephi 30:1(2)
Ether 4:1(3), 2, 3, 5(2)

6 Program Flashcards

Alphabet Flashcards

The pages that follow can be removed and laminated to use as flashcards. They may also be copied, or enlarged, and printed on cardstock. If this is done, it is suggested that the uppercase letters be copied on a different color of paper from the lowercase letters.

a	b
c	d
e	f
g	h

by	and
do	came
for	end
he	great

i	j
k	l
m	n
o	p

judge	in
land	king
not	my
pass	on

q	r
s	t
u	v
w	x

reign	quiet
to	said
have	unto
exceed	were

y	z

zion	ye

A	B
C	D
E	F
G	H

By	And
Do	Came
For	End
He	Great

I	J
K	L
M	N
O	P

Judge	In
Land	King
Not	My
Pass	On

Q	R
S	T
U	V
W	X

Reign	Quiet
To	Said
Have	Unto
Exceed	Were

Y	Z

Zion	Ye

Phonics
Flashcards

The pages that follow can be removed and laminated to use as flashcards. They may also be copied, or enlarged, and printed on cardstock. If this is done, it is suggested that the uppercase letters be copied on a different color of paper from the lowercase letters.

ā	a
c	ē
g	ī
o	ō

a̲lso	āngel
ēagle	c̲ity
ī̲dol	g̲entile
ōr	who̲

$\underline{o}$	$\underline{s}$
$\underline{u}$	$\underline{u}$
$\underline{x}$	$\underline{y}$
$\underline{y}$	

i<u>s</u>	<u>o</u>f
p<u>u</u>t	ū̱se
mȳ	<u>X</u>erxes
	man<u>y</u>

Ā	A̲
C̲	Ē
G̲	Ī
O̲	Ō

<u>A</u>lso	Āngel
Ēagle	<u>C</u>ity
Īdol	<u>G</u>entile
Ōr	Wh<u>o</u>

O	S
U	U
X	Y
Y	

I<u>s</u>	<u>O</u>f
P<u>u</u>t	$\overline{U}$se
M<u>ȳ</u>	<u>X</u>erxes
	Man<u>y</u>

Number
Flashcards

The pages that follow can be removed and laminated to use as flashcards. They may also be copied, or enlarged, and printed on cardstock.

0	1
2	3
4	5
6	7

8	9
10	11
12	13
14	15

16	17
18	19
20	25
30	35

40	45
50	60
70	80
90	100

21	22
23	24
26	27
28	29

31	32
33	34
36	37
38	39

41	42
43	44
46	47
48	49

Word
Flashcards

The pages that follow can be removed and laminated to use as flashcards. They may also be copied, or enlarged, and printed on cardstock. If this is done, it is suggested that the uppercase letters be copied on a different color of paper from the lowercase letters.

I	A
Of	To
And	The
In	It

That	They
Unto	He
Be	For
Not	His

All	Alma
Nephi	Them
Came	Pass
Were	God

Had	Lord
Which	There
Shall	Did
My	Ye

Is	Now
Was	Yea
Have	With
This	By

People	Behold
Who	But
Also	Upon
Him	Are

Land	Should

a	of
to	and
the	in
it	that

they	unto
he	be
for	not
his	all

them	came
pass	were
god	had
lord	which

there	shall
did	my
ye	is
now	was

yea	have
with	this
by	people
behold	who

but	also
upon	him
are	land
should	

Top 50

words in the Book of Mormon in the order to be taught

1. I
2. a
3. of
4. to
5. and
6. the
7. in
8. it
9. that
10. they
11. unto
12. he
13. be
14. for
15. not
16. his
17. all
18. Alma
19. Nephi
20. them
21. came
22. pass
23. were
24. God
25. had
26. Lord
27. which
28. their
29. shall
30. did
31. my
32. ye
33. is
34. now
35. was
36. yea
37. have
38. with
39. this
40. by
41. people
42. behold
43. who
44. but
45. also
46. upon
47. him
48. are
49. land
50. should

About the Author

Vicki Rasmussen was born in San Francisco and grew up in the Bay Area. She studied at Brigham Young University, both in Provo and Hawaii. She enjoys tutoring reading in various community groups and has worked as an elementary school teacher's aide in literacy. She currently serves on the advisory board to the Box Elder County Literacy Program and enjoys rural life in Northern Utah. She and her husband are the parents of seven children.

Vicki is also the author of *The True Story of "The Night Before Christmas,"* an illustrated children's book.